Date: 1/19/22

BR 599.41392 NIL
Nilsen, Genevieve,
Bat pups /

TOOLS FOR CAREGIVERS

- **F&P LEVEL:** D
- **WORD COUNT:** 42
- **CURRICULUM CONNECTIONS:** animals, habitats

Skills to Teach

- **HIGH-FREQUENCY WORDS:** a, are, her, in, is, it, on, she, they, this, what
- **CONTENT WORDS:** baby, bats, big, called, colony, flies, hang(s), holds, group, live, Mom's, pups, sleep, small, tree, upside down, wings
- **PUNCTUATION:** exclamation points, periods, question mark
- **WORD STUDY:** long /e/, spelled ee (*sleep*, *tree*); long /e/, spelled *y* (*baby*, *colony*); long /i/, spelled *ie* (*flies*); /ow/, spelled *ow* (*down*)
- **TEXT TYPE:** factual description

Before Reading Activities

- Read the title and give a simple statement of the main idea.
- Have students "walk" through the book and talk about what they see in the pictures.
- Introduce new vocabulary by having students predict the first letter and locate the word in the text.
- Discuss any unfamiliar concepts that are in the text.

After Reading Activities

Talk with the readers about bat features. Explain to them that bats are mammals. They are the only mammals that can fly! They have wings. What other animals with wings can students name? Ask the readers to think of how bats and birds are similar and different.

Tadpole Books are published by Jump!, 5357 Penn Avenue South, Minneapolis, MN 55419, www.jumplibrary.com

Copyright ©2022 Jump. International copyright reserved in all countries. No part of this book may be reproduced in any form without written permission from the publisher.

Editor: Jenna Gleisner **Designer:** Molly Ballanger

Photo Credits: Doug Gimesy/Nature Picture Library, cover; Nico Faramaz/Shutterstock, 1; Sstoll850/Dreamstime, 3; CraigRJD/iStock, 2ml, 4–5; Somakram/Dreamstime, 2tl, 6–7; DanieleC/Alamy, 2bl, 8–9; Passakorn Umpornmaha/Shutterstock, 2br, 10–11; CHANUN.V/Shutterstock, 2tr, 12–13; Nature Picture Library/Alamy, 2mr, 14–15; Independent birds/Shutterstock, 16.

Library of Congress Cataloging-in-Publication Data
Names: Nilsen, Genevieve, author.
Title: Bat pups / by Genevieve Nilsen.
Description: Minneapolis: Jump!, Inc., (2022) | Series: Outback babies | Includes index. | Audience: Ages 3–6
Identifiers: LCCN 2020047183 (print) | LCCN 2020047184 (ebook) | ISBN 9781645279372 (hardcover)
ISBN 9781645279389 (paperback) | ISBN 9781645279396 (ebook)
Subjects: LCSH: Bats—Infancy—Juvenile literature.
Classification: LCC QL737.C5 N55 2022 (print) | LCC QL737.C5 (ebook) | DDC 599.4139/2—dc23
LC record available at https://lccn.loc.gov/2020047183
LC ebook record available at https://lccn.loc.gov/2020047184

BAT PUPS

by Genevieve Nilsen

TABLE OF CONTENTS

Words to Know 2

Bat Pups 3

Let's Review! 16

Index 16

tadpole
books

WORDS TO KNOW

colony

flies

hangs

holds

pups

wings

BAT PUPS

What hangs in this tree?

bat

Bats!

They live in a group.

It is called a colony.

pup

Baby bats are called pups.

Pups are small.

wing

Mom's wings are big.

She flies.

Her pup holds on!

They hang upside down.

They sleep!

15

LET'S REVIEW!

What are this bat pup and its mom doing?

INDEX

colony 7

flies 11

hangs 3, 14

holds 13

pups 8, 9, 13

sleep 15

tree 3

wings 10